Exploring the West

Contents

Lesson 1: Daniel Boone 2
Lesson 2: The Louisiana Purchase 6
Lesson 3: Lewis and Clark 9
Lesson 4: Sacagawea 13

1 Daniel Boone

Young Daniel Boone grew up in the forests.
He made friends with the Indians.
They taught him how to hunt wild animals.

Daniel Boone hunted to feed his family.
He always carried his favorite rifle, or gun.

Daniel Boone heard stories about Kentucky. He wanted to explore this beautiful land.

This picture shows the Wilderness Road. It is the path that Daniel Boone and his friends made to reach Kentucky.

2 The Louisiana Purchase

This family is traveling to New Orleans, Louisiana, on a flatboat.
They are on the Mississippi River.

This painting shows the city of New Orleans in 1803.
It was a busy French trading port.

The United States bought New Orleans and much more land from France.
It was called the Louisiana Purchase.

Lewis and Clark 3

These men are Meriwether Lewis and William Clark. President Jefferson sent them to explore the West.

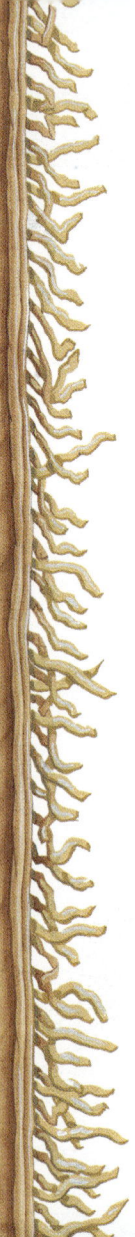

Lewis and Clark's trip was dangerous. Sometimes bears chased them.

Lewis and Clark sailed up the Missouri River. The river may have looked like this.

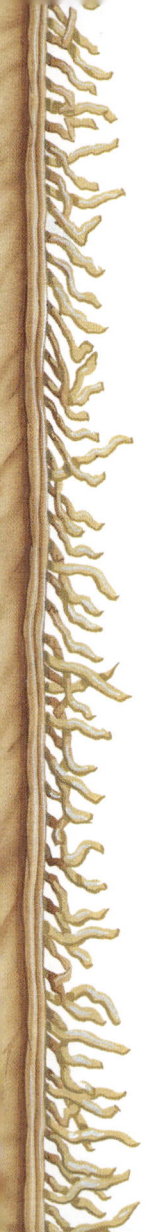

Lewis and Clark climbed over the Rocky Mountains.
The snow and rain made the trip hard.

Sacagawea 4

Sacagawea lived near the Rocky Mountains. She liked to pick berries in the woods.

Sacagawea traveled with Lewis and Clark. Her baby rode on her back in a cradleboard.

1961.195. Charles M. Russell. "Lewis and Clark on the Lower Columbia," watercolor, gouache and graphite on paper, 1905. Amon Carter Museum, Fort Worth, Texas.

Sacagawea was Lewis and Clark's guide. She talked with other Native Americans and helped make peace.

Today Sacagawea is remembered for her bravery.